NANCY CROW

IMPROVISATIONAL QUILTS

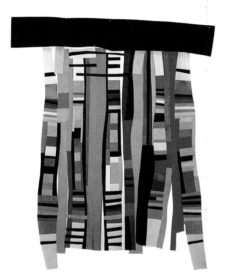

Renwick Gallery of The National Museum of American Art
Smithsonian Institution, Washington, D.C.
August 25, 1995, to January 1, 1996

C&T PUBLISHING

Dedicated to my Mother RACHEL KENSETT CROW (1899-1984)
"We are doing it!"

5 4 3 2 1

in photographing my work over the past seven years. My hand quilters: Marla Hattabaugh, Kris Doyle, Marie Moore, Sue Milling, Brenda Stultz, Anna Marie Gazo, Mary Underwood, and Suzanne Keller for bindings and embroidered titles. Louise O. Townsend, my editor; Liz Aneloski, my technical editor; Jill Berry, my graphic designer; Diane Pedersen, my editorial design director; Todd and Tony Hensley, co-owners of C&T Publishing; The Renwick Gallery, and Michael Monroe, its director.

Acknowledgments:
I wish to thank the following people for their support: My husband, John Stitzlein, and my two sons, Nathaniel Crow Stitzlein and Matthew Crow Stitzlein, for their strong love and support. Penny McMorris for believing in me. Penny McMorris, Ann Batchelder, Sandra Blain, and Paul J. Smith for writing the statements included in this catalogue. J Kevin Fitzsimons, staff photographer at The Ohio State University, for his patience and loyalty

"Aspire to inspire ere you expire."

—Birdie Lusch, Ohio Outsider Artist (deceased)

Why the need to be remembered? Where did the drive come from that pushes relentlessly; that has pushed relentlessly ever since I was young? The drive that exacerbated my oft times depressive moods when I was in my 20s and 30s—when I did not know what I was doing or wanted to do or how to do it. The drive never let up. It was ever forceful and guilt-provoking, always heckling me to get focused, to get disciplined, to quit wasting precious time, to start making difficult decisions about what and who would have to be cut out of my life so that work would always be first. It was drive that insisted I start the long apprenticeship in learning wherein one must practice and practice and practice and begin to answer the mystery of how to become one with the medium. It soon became very clear to me that nearly every obstruction with few exceptions could fall under the mantle of procrastination. So procrastination had to be thoroughly examined, understood, and ruthlessly dealt with.

Earlier on, I had encouraged dialogues with other talented people about their dedication to their art forms. But so often these dialogues lapsed into excuse-making sessions about why work was not getting done or even made. Suddenly I realized, who cares? Who cares about work that never gets made? Who cares about talents never used or fulfilled? The only thing that matters in the end is that the talent has evolved, has been nourished, and that a legacy has been left behind. Millions of excuses do not create legacies.

I have always thought long and hard about what I wanted to accomplish with my work. What became apparent was that I wanted to reach a state where work would flow out of me unimpeded, freely, joyously, and that it would represent whoever I am and my experiences. Long ago I quit caring that fabric was not a particularly acceptable medium in the art world because caring meant a denial of what I loved. This relaxed attitude released a lot of energy. It seemed to me that the only way to work was to think of fabric as my ally.

I have always been a person of high energy with enormous, intense feelings about everything in life. I understand the energy of exaggeration, and I use the intensity of exaggeration in my speech and my work. I have spent hours staring out the window of my studio at the branches of the mature apple trees in my orchard. Sinuously the branches curve off in irregular lines in all directions. The effect is very dramatic, and I react with pounding heartbeats! Is this what Van Gogh might have seen, I ask myself? His drawings reflect his love of beautiful linear shapes. Why did he love linear shapes so much? Why do I love linear shapes so much? Why do I always take time to observe and absorb the formations of the branches against the winter sky? The beauty of all of these incredibly sensuous branches offers me hope during the long hard winters. The beauty helps me stay centered.

I like constructions—pieces and parts of shapes all fitting together somehow. I admire all types of constructions: well-designed buildings, beautiful roof lines, Chinese tile roofs, timber frame barns, thick brick walls, small panes of glass with wooden mullions, huge wooden porches, fancy gingerbread trims, massive stone foundations, brick streets, slate roofs, trellisses—constructions. As a child, I thought I would scream with frustration everytime my brother dragged out our large box of lincoln logs. I hated those boring brown logs, all the same color, all similar shapes. Anything I built always fell apart! Boring! But somehow they managed to affect me because I know now that I must (that I need to) put my fabric shapes together as constructions, as wooden pieces that join together. Only the shapes must be exaggerated and lyrical and spontaneously cut of limitless colors. And where the shapes join together? Can something miraculous happen there, too?

I am what I call a random thinker in that I am attracted to an idea before I have even begun to think through the last idea and so on until I become overwhelmed. That is why I must use sets and variables. I have to start somewhere. And the way I work today forces me to take an enormous number of things that are sort of dangling in the air or in my brain and put them into some kind of form that makes sense!

So why am I working improvisationally now? Why did it take me so long to arrive at this point? Quiltmaking has its own history of techniques that are frankly obsessive, unrelenting and too time-consuming for most people or just too tedious for today's hurried-up lifestyle. As a child, I loved the processes of cut-paper work and gluing cut-outs onto another sheet of paper. It follows that I loved cutting shapes out of fabric and piecing those shapes together. As I developed greater sophistication in creating forms, I longed for a way to work that did not involve rigid pattern-making. I wanted a more direct way to create those shapes so that my compositions could dance with a magic freshness. I read everything I could find on Van Gogh's and Cézanne's need to find a way to express themselves with their medium of painting. I, too, needed my own individual way to express myself directly with the fabric, a way that included no barriers. So I plunged in and began to practice, and I kept practicing until I taught myself to cut shapes directly out of the fabric without templates, without even knowing ahead of time what the overall composition might be. I quickly knew I was on track because I was in love with quiltmaking again. Five years before, I was ready to give it up because I could not tolerate the tedium involved.

So now I cut a shape and pin it up on my great white void of a work-wall. I react! I cut another shape and pin it up. I don't like it, and I throw it away. Without hesitation I cut another shape and another and on and on, pinning and trying and moving shapes around. Struggle with relationships and keep going. No excuses, no procrastination. No time to waste. Just feel the joy and liberation! Become one with the fabric; feel its rhythms; understand the medium! Everything leads to freedom! Push the fabric. Be direct. It's who I am. I am direct. No time for hesitation. Too old for that. And who cares really? Only I do. And then only the final work speaks and stays as a reminder of what was nourished.

Nancy Crow
February 1995
Baltimore, Ohio

3

Nancy Crow works now like a great jazz musician

to whom the basic chords are second nature. She plays freshly with the themes that quilters have developed over time. This one-woman exhibition shows her in transition, leaving the comfortable familiarity of knowing what to play, what to risk again, and what to simply improvise.

These quilts seem formed from two moods: joy and struggle. The joy—the passion she finds in work, in feeling fabric, creating colors, shapes and patterns, locking out the world to dig deep within her soul. The struggle is to stay there; to keep out doubt, avoid the easy, risk her reputation simply to satisfy herself. Her goal is just to keep her fire burning, to make work she can learn from as she tries to understand herself.

Inquisitive by nature, Nancy reads a lot and asks blunt questions. She wants to know how other artists feel, how they keep going; how women balance family life with art. She herself is often asked one question: "Why quilts and why not paintings?"—as if the medium she works in somehow defines the worth of what she does.

And the answer? Let Nancy tell the story of the quilt by Sarah Dunn that changed the focus of her own art:

> I remember my visit to the home of Berenice Dunlap sometime during 1973 when I first began to be interested in looking at quilts. I never really thought about quilts before then…. Berenice told me about an antique quilt in her cedar chest, and I asked to see it…. Out of the cedar chest came the most stunning quilt I had ever seen! My heart pounded!

It was like seeing a modern painting emerging from that trunk. Sharp red and soft green triangles stood out against a black wool field, in 13 Bear's Paw blocks made 70 years earlier.

> The impact of that quilt changed my life. I could not get over the boldness, the beauty of the wool fabrics, the immense simplicity of design, and the beautiful craftsmanship. The use of black…against red…all that black. So much black! How could Sarah Dunn have been so daring to use so much black? Especially when the quilt was intended for a baby?

Nancy was already quilting by then. She would sit in with quilters down at the Senior Citizens' Center in Cambridge, Ohio. But she found it just a useful pastime, like knitting. Weaving was her art—what she had studied for her MFA. But that quilt! "Somewhere in my brain, it clicked that quilts could be very, very great…."

When her family (husband John Stitzlein and sons Nathaniel and Matthew) moved to Athens, Ohio, she felt drawn toward quiltmaking and found like-minded friends. "It was like a suction…a need. All of us wanted to do quilts…. We were hungry for everything we could find on quilts in books or magazines."

Nancy's time in Athens was, in a way, like going back to school. Only now these new quilters met weekly to teach and critique themselves, reworking classic patterns like Log Cabin. I saw some of their quilts back in 1976. And Nancy's jolted me with the same shock she had felt from Sarah Dunn. I knew she'd grow to greatness. My own quilts never interested me again.

In 1979, Nancy and her family moved once more, trading Athens' active college town life for rural Baltimore, Ohio. Nancy's reaction? "My first response to the farm was, 'Oh, how romantic!' That response reversed itself within days. I think I was truly horrified to find that the long lane in front of our house was accurately symbolic. We were cut off from the world!"

They say what doesn't kill you makes you stronger. Nancy's isolation brought depression and plunged her deeper into work. By now, she had packed away her loom and focused only on quilts. And within a year, she found the world quite literally beating a path down that long country lane to see her work. New York City curators called, asking if she would come out and show. The Museum of American Folk Art added her work to their collection. The American Craft Museum placed a quilt of hers (*March Study*, shown below) front and center in their window and even on the cover of their magazine. And that was nearly 15 years ago.

Now, here she is at mid-career, still struggling to make her work express the deep emotions and the conflicts that she feels. She hears the clock now. She's tightrope walking—daring to move ever farther out from solid ground.

"I feel as though I'm touching something inside myself that's so emotional and overwhelming that I've given up part of my life, and as it goes, I'm afraid it will be gone forever," she says. It's true that she has never worked so freely. She's not preplanning—trusting chance, instead. Cutting into fabric, she lets her heart determine where her hand will go.

"It was so difficult to come to the point in my life where I gave myself permission to release," she says, explaining this new freedom with a sense of both exhilaration and fright. "All I know is that I want to go in the direction my heart and mind lead me."

Whatever the outcome of this exhibition, one thing is clear. Nancy Crow is the artist who will define what quiltmaking was like in our time, long after she, and we, are gone. And what will they say about her? Perhaps the words that Nancy heard from Sarah Dunn's quilt: "I am a strong individual, and you will know that I am here, that I have been."

Penny McMorris

Art Curator for Owens-Corning Fiberglas Corporation; partner in the Electric Quilt Company; and producer of the PBS television series, "The Great American Quilt" Bowling Green, *Ohio*

4

Nancy Crow is a maverick.

She is not afraid to speak her mind, to go against popular trends in her field, to stretch the boundaries of her medium. Her contributions to the art quilt movement can best be appreciated by understanding how both her art and her personality have influenced an entire generation of artists.

What distinguishes Crow's work is her willingness to take risks within a formal art aesthetic. She was one of the first artists to clearly break from traditional quiltmaking without mimicking another art form, such as painting, yet color and composition are primary concerns in her art.

Crow's work is not merely an exercise in technical tricks or clever interpretations of a given formula—it is an expression of her soul's struggles. Through her quilts, she speaks about pain, depression, freedom, joy. In her words, a quilt "has to sing!" It is her exuberance, her passion that gives life to her work.

Nancy Crow is a mentor. In her classes, workshops, lectures, and writings, she pushes quilters to reconsider their work within a broader art arena. Her classes emphasize content, color, and design over technique. She encourages students to find (and use) their own voices. At the same time, she is deeply committed to the process, the making of her art.

Nancy Crow is a pioneer. As she says, "Twenty years ago, there were so few people penetrating [the fiber art field]…it was just like going out and settling California or Oregon." When galleries were unwilling to exhibit art quilts, Crow secured a major venue for these new works. In 1979 the first Quilt National was exhibited at The Dairy Barn Cultural Arts Center in Athens, Ohio. This important biennial, juried show has expanded and now travels internationally, creating a vital network of artists and collectors.

Nancy Crow is an innovator. Fascinated by color, Crow wanted to ignite interest among quilters in designing their own fabrics. Until this point, most art quilts relied on commercial cloths. In 1990, she established the annual Quilt/Surface Design Symposium. Every summer an increasingly diverse faculty of quilt and surface design professionals gathers to teach and exchange ideas. As a result, the majority of art quilt exhibitions today display a significant number of quilts incorporating original fabric designs.

Innovation is also seen in Crow's art. Her recent quilts, centering on a theme of improvisation, speak to the artist's increasing sense of freedom—a spontaneity springing from self-confidence held deep within. It is her belief in her creative process and in the quilt format as a vehicle for this expression that keeps her work fresh. An exceptional artist, Nancy Crow deserves recognition not only for what she has accomplished but for what she has enabled and inspired others to do.

Ann Batchelder, Editor
FIBERARTS Magazine
Asheville, North Carolina

Contemporary quiltmaking represents one of the most vital areas of fiber art in the United States today. Over the past two decades, this art, so strongly rooted in tradition, has been infused with new energy and vision by American artists. Few of them have been more influential in establishing the place of the new "art quilt" or expanding its artistic horizons than Nancy Crow.

Nancy Crow was a pioneer in developing a new aesthetic for the modern quilt. In the early 1970s, she departed from tapestry weaving to explore assemblage of fabric. Using traditional quiltmaking skills, she began to create work that transcended the classic quilt form and placed the art of quiltmaking in new perspective. Each piece in the continuous series that she has since created connects to those that came before it while exploring new concepts.

One of the strongest aspects of Nancy Crow's work is her exceptional talent in manipulating color. In each piece, she redefines color relationships in complex geometric patterns that create magical kaleidoscopic effects. These visual fantasies combine richness of fabric, meticulous craftsmanship, and a strong graphic order. Their powerful presence reflects her deep sensitivity to the beauty of life and the experiences she encounters daily and on her travels throughout the world.

Nancy Crow's work is also characterized by a tremendous energy that reflects her own lifestyle and personality. With equal skill and creativity, she orchestrates her family and social life, her business career, her teaching, and a vast network of international activities.

This collection, which represents her latest work, celebrates the art of quiltmaking on its highest level, and pays tribute to one of the outstanding fiber artists of our time.

Paul J. Smith, Director Emeritus
American Craft Museum
New York City

This catalog and the exhibition it documents celebrate the career of an extraordinary quilt artist and teacher. Nancy Crow's role in the contemporization of quilts in this country and her importance as a teacher cannot be understated. Nancy has led the quilt revolution that began in the mid-1970s and irrevocably transformed the perception of quilts from solely functional forms to true art pieces.

Nancy's work characterizes the diversity of art quilts conveying the depth of personal content that is distinctive of someone of her stature in the art world. Her quilts are her life, thus her voice. Referencing her heritage and the quilt tradition, she uses known techniques, liberally combining materials and processes and inventing surfaces utilizing seemingly elemental shapes rich in color and pattern. Nancy's quilts epitomize an artist with great visionary depth articulating powerful abstracted images echoing her past and staging her future.

Teaching is a critical part of Nancy's life. For years, students at Arrowmont School of Arts and Crafts have been enriched through the sharing of Nancy's work concepts and motivational abilities. She thrives in an environment of intensity and connection where students' growth is witnessed by their inclusion in exhibitions, in print materials, and in teaching. These artists are now re-defining the boundaries of art quilts as Nancy herself continues to do.

Sandra Blain, Director
Arrowmont School of Arts and Crafts
Gatlinburg, Tennessee

The Linear Study Series concentrates on creating linear configurations by cutting directly into the fabrics without use of templates or preparation drawings. Most of the sewing was done without pinning even though much curved work was involved.

Left: DETAIL: LINEAR STUDY #4

Above: LINEAR STUDY #1

24" x 24"   ©1993 Nancy Crow
Solid-color pima cottons hand-dyed by Nancy Crow.
Center square resist-dyed by Lunn Fabrics.
Fabrics cut into directly and pieced by Nancy Crow.
Hand-quilted by Marla Hattabaugh.

Far Right: LINEAR STUDY #4

15¾" x 53½"   ©1995 Nancy Crow
All pima cottons hand-dyed by Nancy Crow.
Fabrics cut into directly and pieced by Nancy Crow.
Hand-quilted by Marla Hattabaugh.

Right: ARTIST'S STUDIO

Nancy Crow in her basement dyeing/painting studio
preparing fabric to be used in her Linear Study Series,
1995. This workspace is 25' x 25' and contains a large
stainless steel three-hole sink, washing machine and
dryer, and two large work tables that can be used for
monoprinting and painting.

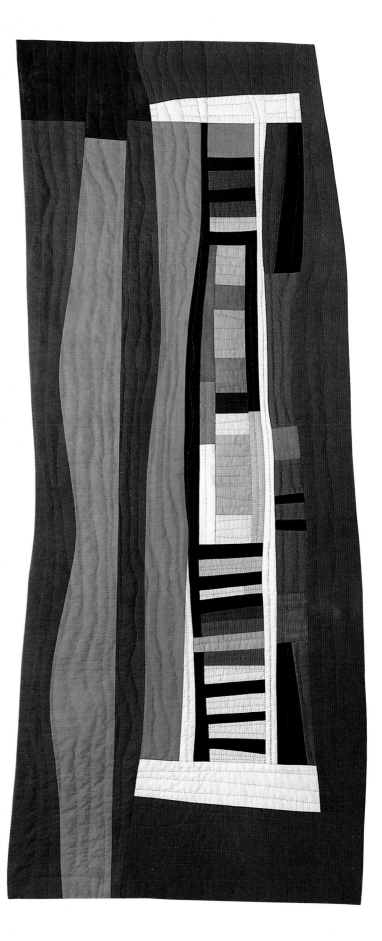

Left: LINEAR STUDY #3
49" x 57"   ©1994-1995 Nancy Crow
100% cotton fabrics hand-dyed by Nancy Crow.
Fabrics cut into directly and pieced by Nancy Crow.
Hand-quilted by Marla Hattabaugh.

Above: LINEAR STUDY #2
26" x 26"   ©1994 Nancy Crow
Solid-color pima cottons hand-dyed by Nancy Crow.
Center square resist-dyed by Lunn Fabrics.
Fabrics cut into directly and pieced by Nancy Crow.
Hand-quilted by Marla Hattabaugh.

Right: LINEAR STUDY #5
18" x 47"   ©1995 Nancy Crow
All pima cottons hand-dyed by Nancy Crow.
Fabrics cut into directly and pieced by Nancy Crow.
Hand-quilted by Kris Doyle.

Color Blocks #52 and #54 were studies for Color Blocks #56. The fabrics were cut directly without templates and inserted as floaters.

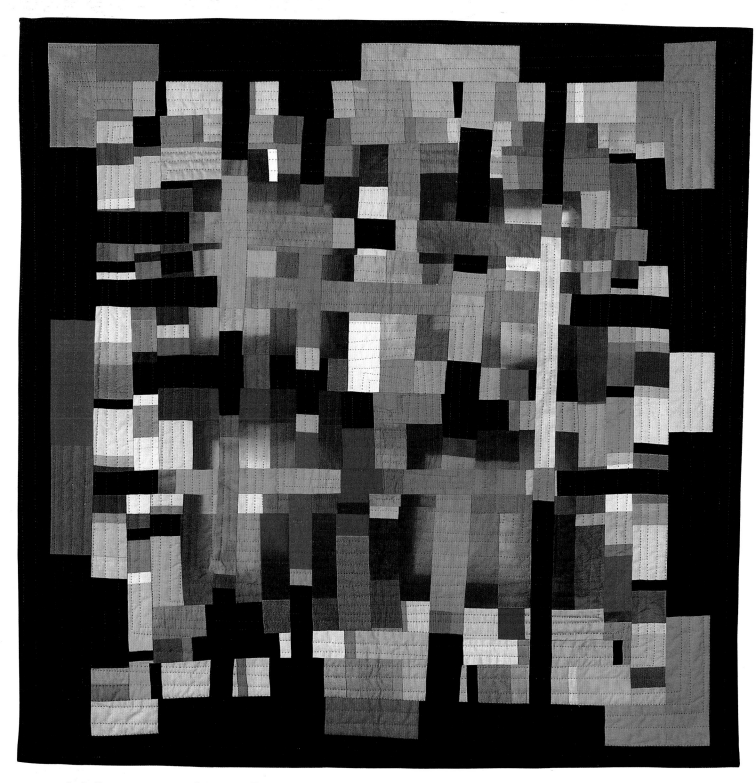

Left: DETAIL OF COLOR BLOCKS #54

Above: COLOR BLOCKS #54

32½" x 33¼"   ©1994 Nancy Crow
Pima cottons hand-dyed by Nancy Crow.
Resist-dyed fabrics by Lunn Fabrics.
Cut and machine-pieced by Nancy Crow.
Hand-quilted by Marla Hattabaugh.

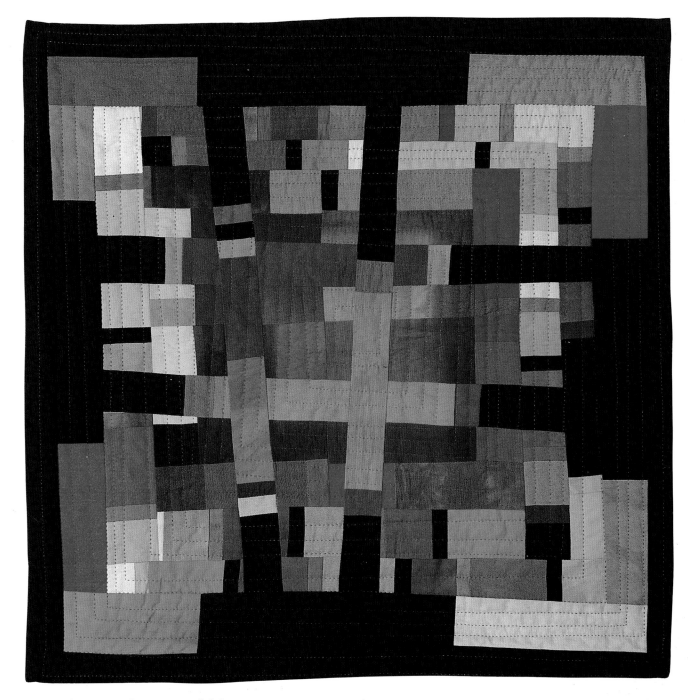

Above: C O L O R   B L O C K S   # 5 2

22" x 22"   ©1994 Nancy Crow
Pima cottons hand-dyed by Nancy Crow.
Resist-dyed fabrics by Lunn Fabrics.
Cut and machine-pieced by Nancy Crow.
Hand-quilted by Marla Hattabaugh.

Right: C O L O R   B L O C K S   # 5 6

69½" x 70½"   ©1994 Nancy Crow
Cottons hand-dyed by Lunn Fabrics and Nancy Crow.
Hand-quilted by Marla Hattabaugh.
Cut and machine-pieced by Nancy Crow.
Private collection.

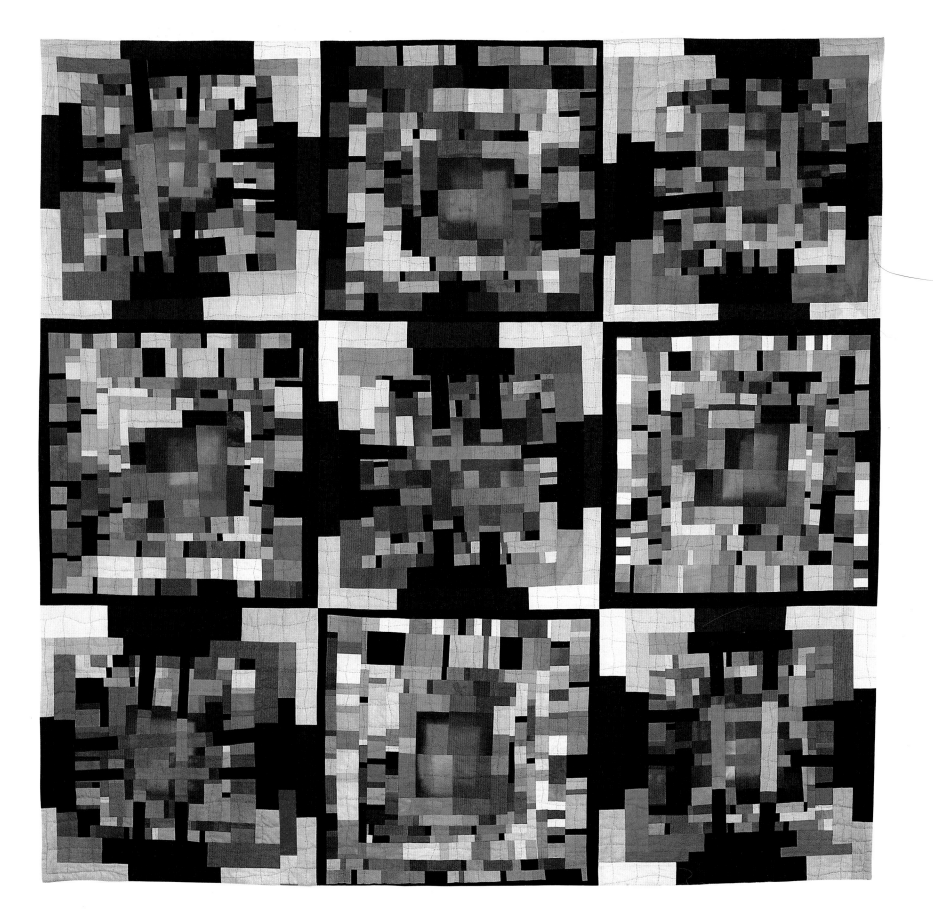

Color Blocks #25-35: 1 live on a farm where all the outbuildings are timber frame structures built in the late 1800s. Over a three-year period my husband and two sons dismantled and moved a huge 1884 timber frame barn to our farm. During the next two years, they rebuilt the barn, and this process had enormous influence on my quilt construction. In some sense, I feel the parts of these quilts are like boards fitting together. The Color Blocks series are all 100% cotton materials. All quilts were cut out and machine-pieced by Nancy Crow

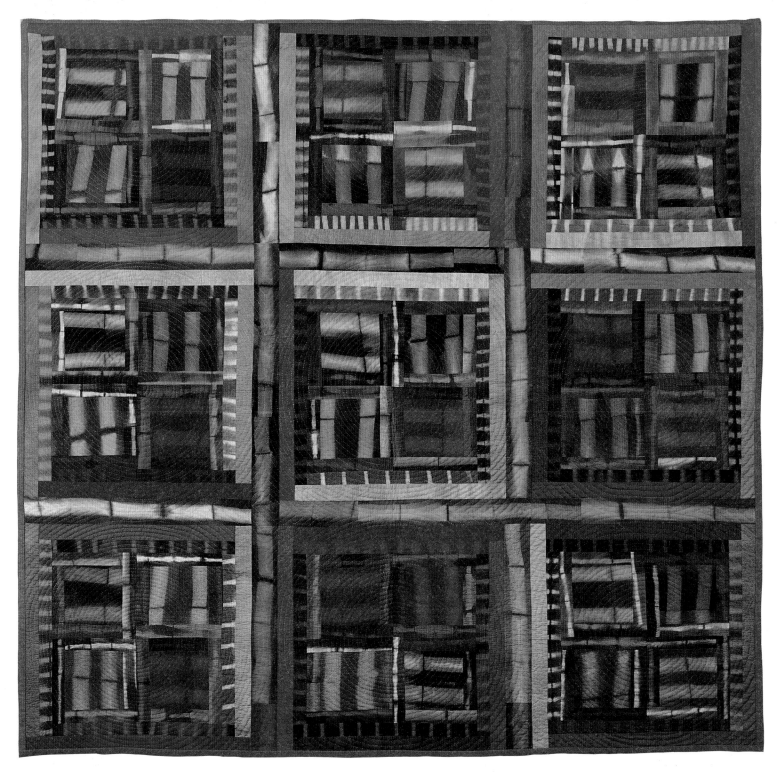

Left: DETAIL OF COLOR BLOCKS #25

Above: COLOR BLOCKS #25

68" x 68"   ©1992 Nancy Crow
Cottons hand-dyed, resist-dyed by Lunn Fabrics.
Cut and machine-pieced by Nancy Crow.
Hand-quilted by Marie Moore with pattern denoted by
Nancy Crow.

Above: C O L O R   B L O C K S   # 2 6

64" x 64"   ©1992 Nancy Crow
Cottons hand-dyed, resist-dyed by Lunn Fabrics,
Nancy Crow, and Eric Morti.
Cut and machine-pieced by Nancy Crow.
Hand-quilted by Brenda Stultz with pattern denoted by
Nancy Crow.

Right: C O L O R   B L O C K S   # 2 7

68" x 68"   ©1992 Nancy Crow
Cottons hand-dyed, resist-dyed by Lunn Fabrics,
Nancy Crow, and Eric Morti.
Cut and machine-pieced by Nancy Crow.
Hand-quilted by Marla Hattabaugh with pattern
denoted by Nancy Crow.

18

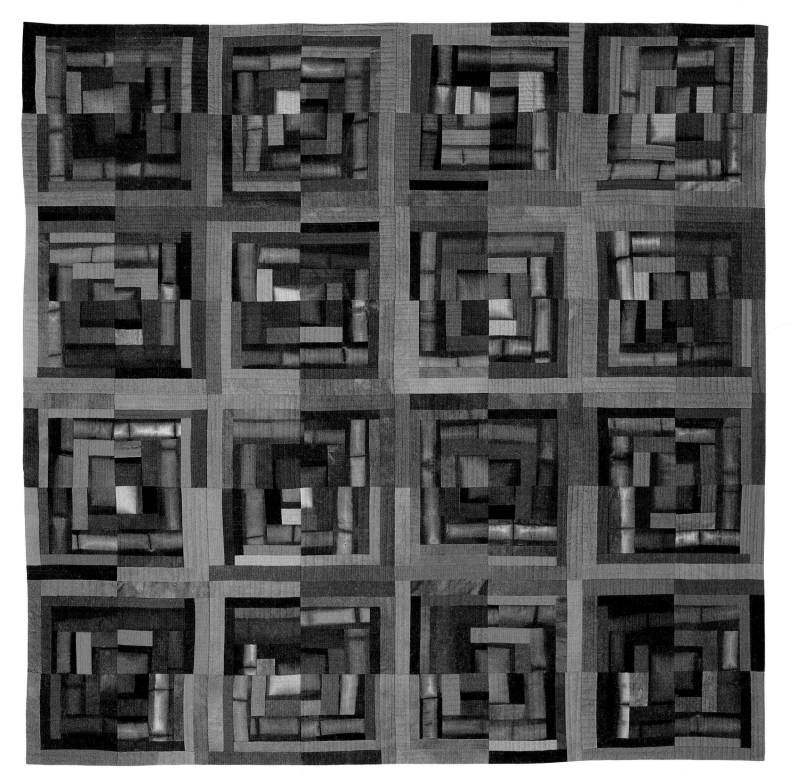

Above: COLOR BLOCKS #23

72" x 72"   ©1992 Nancy Crow
Cottons and pima cottons hand-dyed by Nancy Crow,
Lunn Fabrics and Eric Morti.
Cut and machine-pieced by Nancy Crow.
Hand-quilted by Marie Moore with pattern denoted by
Nancy Crow.

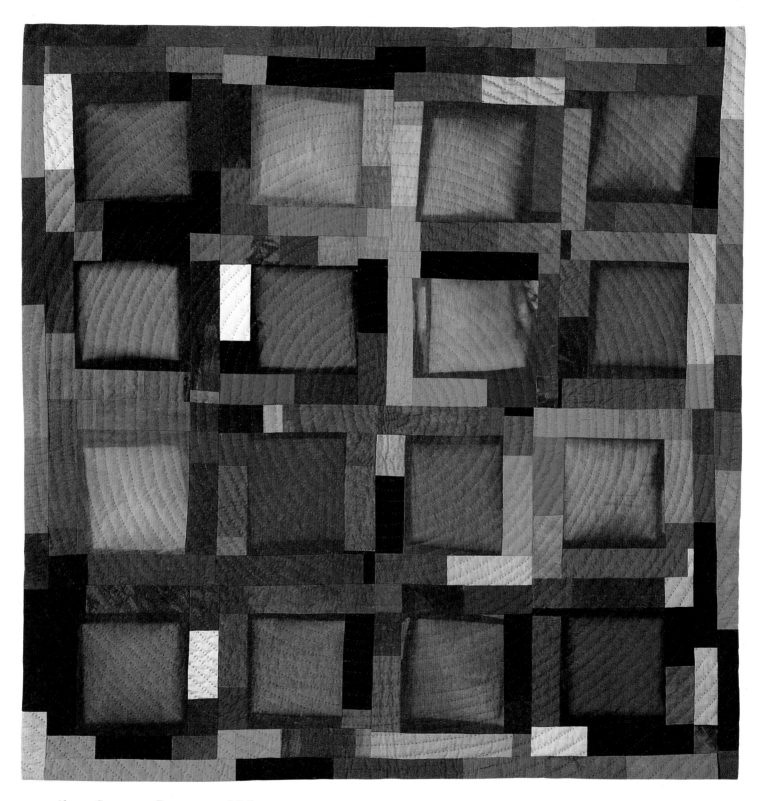

Above: COLOR BLOCKS #35

34½" x 36½"   ©1993 Nancy Crow
Cottons hand-dyed by Lunn Fabrics and Nancy Crow.
Cut and machine-pieced by Nancy Crow.
Hand-quilted by Marie Moore with pattern denoted by
Nancy Crow.

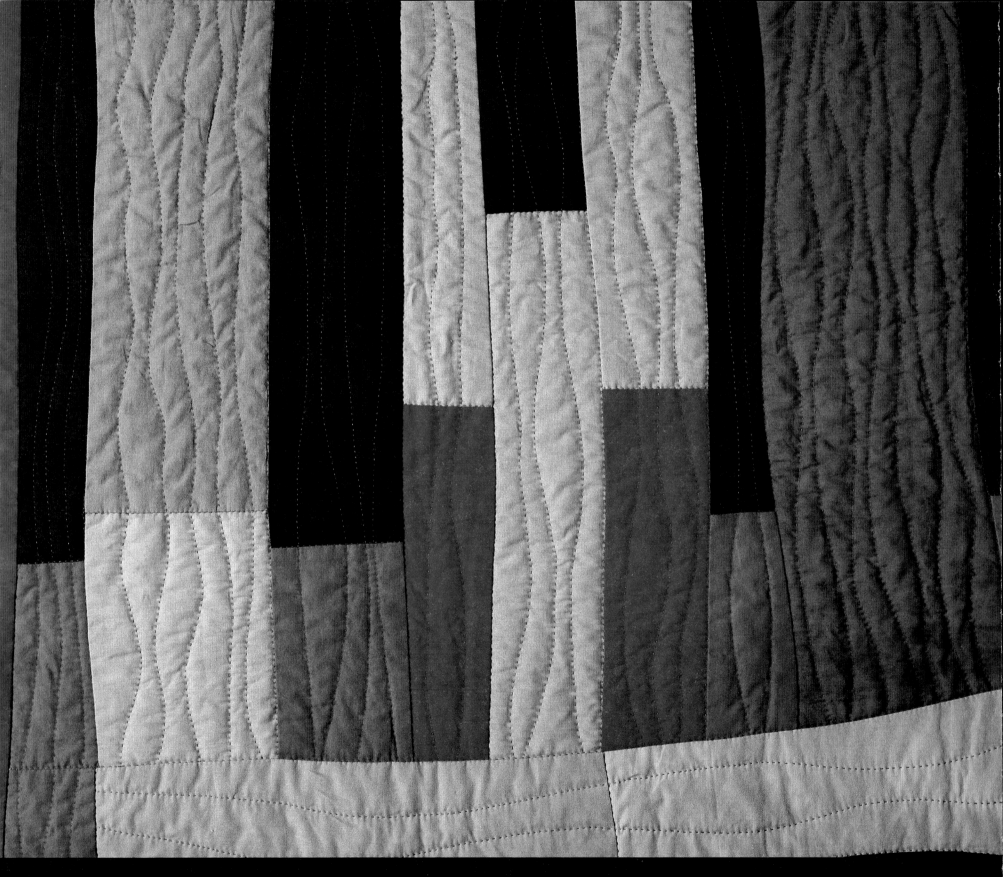

Color Blocks #41, #42, and #55 are all related in that I created them by using my own system of freely cut floaters. No matter how curvilinear the shapes, all were sewn together by direct piecing with no use of appliqué. The composition was determined in process.

Left: D E T A I L C O L O R B L O C K S # 5 5

Above: C O L O R B L O C K S # 5 5

41" x 43"   ©1994 Nancy Crow
Pima cottons hand-dyed by Nancy Crow.
Cut directly from the fabrics and machine-pieced by
Nancy Crow.
No templates or drawings used.
Hand-quilted by Marla Hattabaugh.

Above: C O L O R   B L O C K S   # 4 1

41" x 51"   ©1993-1994 Nancy Crow
Pima cottons hand-dyed by Nancy Crow.
Cut directly from the fabrics and machine-pieced by
Nancy Crow.
No templates or drawings used.
Hand-quilted intensely by Marla Hattabaugh.

Above: C O L O R   B L O C K S   # 4 2

31" x 47"   ©1994 Nancy Crow
Pima cottons hand-dyed by Nancy Crow.
Cut directly from fabrics and machine-pieced by
Nancy Crow.
No templates or drawings used.
Hand-quilted intensely by Kris Doyle.

These Color Blocks quilts are grouped together because they relate to one another in that they are all broken Log Cabins. They were made over a span of two years from 1992-1994. All were made from 100%-cottons, and were cut and pieced without use of templates.

Left: C O L O R   B L O C K S   # 5 1

42" x 44"   ©1994 Nancy Crow
Pima cottons hand-dyed by Nancy Crow. Resist-dyed
fabrics by Lunn Fabrics.
Cut and machine-pieced by Nancy Crow.
No templates used.
Hand-quilted by Marie Moore.
Collection of Mr. and Mrs. Tim Keny.

Above: C O L O R   B L O C K S   # 2 9

53" x 53"   ©1992 Nancy Crow
Fabrics hand-dyed by Nancy Crow with resist-dyed fab-
rics by Lunn Fabrics.
Cut and machine-pieced by Nancy Crow.
No templates used.
Hand-quilted by Sue Milling.

Above: C O L O R   B L O C K S   # 3 0

48" x 48"   ©1992 Nancy Crow
Fabrics hand-dyed by Nancy Crow with resist-dyed
fabrics by Lunn Fabrics.
Cut and machine-pieced by Nancy Crow.
No templates used.
Hand-quilted by Kris Doyle.

Above: C O L O R   B L O C K S   # 3 3

48" x 66"   ©1993 Nancy Crow
Pima cottons hand-dyed by Nancy Crow. Resist-dyed
fabrics by Lunn Fabrics.
Cut and machine-pieced by Nancy Crow.
No templates used.
Hand-quilted by Marla Hattabaugh.

The Bow Tie Series became far more improvisational after Bow Tie #6, as evidenced in Bow Tie #10. And Bow Tie #4 greatly influenced Color Blocks #58. None of this was planned ahead. It just happened!

Left: DETAIL OF BOW TIE #6

Above: BOW TIE #6

71" x 71"   ©1992 Nancy Crow.
Pima cottons hand-dyed by Nancy Crow.
Machine-pieced by Nancy Crow.
Hand-quilted by Marla Hattabaugh with pattern
denoted by Nancy Crow.

Above Left: B O W T I E # 1 0

©1995 Nancy Crow
In-progress (first version in early January 1995) on
large main wall of studio.

Above Right: B O W T I E # 1 0

Approximate size will be 72" x 72"
©1995 Nancy Crow
In-progress (second shot on February 19, 1995), show-
ing some sewing finished. With no templates and so
many irregular shapes, the final sewing is very
slow going!

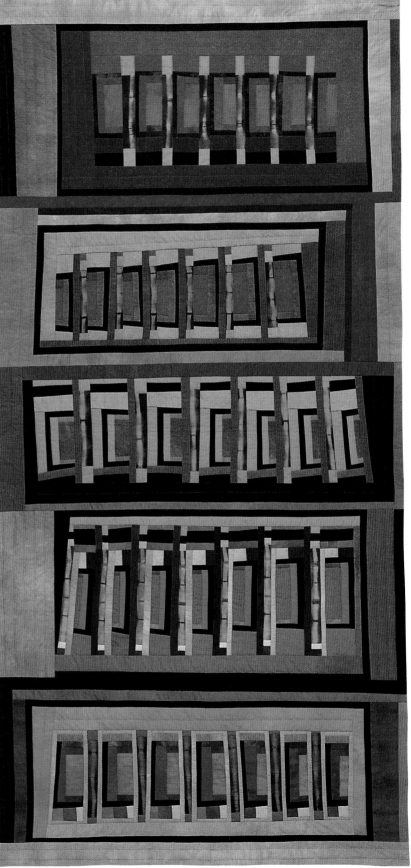

Above: BOW TIE #4

21" x 21"   ©1991 Nancy Crow
100%-cotton fabrics hand-dyed by Eric Morti, Lunn
Fabrics, and Nancy Crow.
Cut and pieced directly by Nancy Crow.
No templates used.
Hand-quilted by Kris Doyle.

Right: COLOR BLOCKS #58

41½" x 88½"   ©1994 Nancy Crow
Pima cottons hand-dyed by Nancy Crow.
Some resist-dyed fabrics by Lunn Fabrics.
Cut and pieced directly by Nancy Crow.
No templates used.
Hand-quilted by Marie Moore.
Collection of Bill and Ruth Lantz.

The Chinese Souls quilts are my memorial to more than 60 teen-age boys who were bound and loaded on huge trucks to be driven to their execution for petty crimes. I witnessed this horrible incident when I was an exchange artist to China in September 1990. The bull's eye embroidery and hand quilting represent the ropes tied around the soul, and all of the colors of circles represent the individuals.

Left: DETAIL OF CHINESE SOULS #6

Above: CHINESE SOULS #2

82" x 90"   ©1992 Nancy Crow
Fabrics hand-dyed and resist-dyed by Lunn Fabrics.
Hand-embroidered by Nancy Crow, Marla Hattabaugh,
Suzanne Keller, and Maria Magisano.
Machine-pieced by Nancy Crow.
Hand-quilted by Marla Hattabaugh with pattern
denoted by Nancy Crow.

Above: C H I N E S E   S O U L S   # 3

70" x 70"   ©1992 Nancy Crow
Fabrics hand-dyed and resist-dyed by Lunn Fabrics,
Eric Morti, and Nancy Crow.
Machine-pieced by Nancy Crow.
Hand-quilted by Sue Milling with pattern denoted by
Nancy Crow.

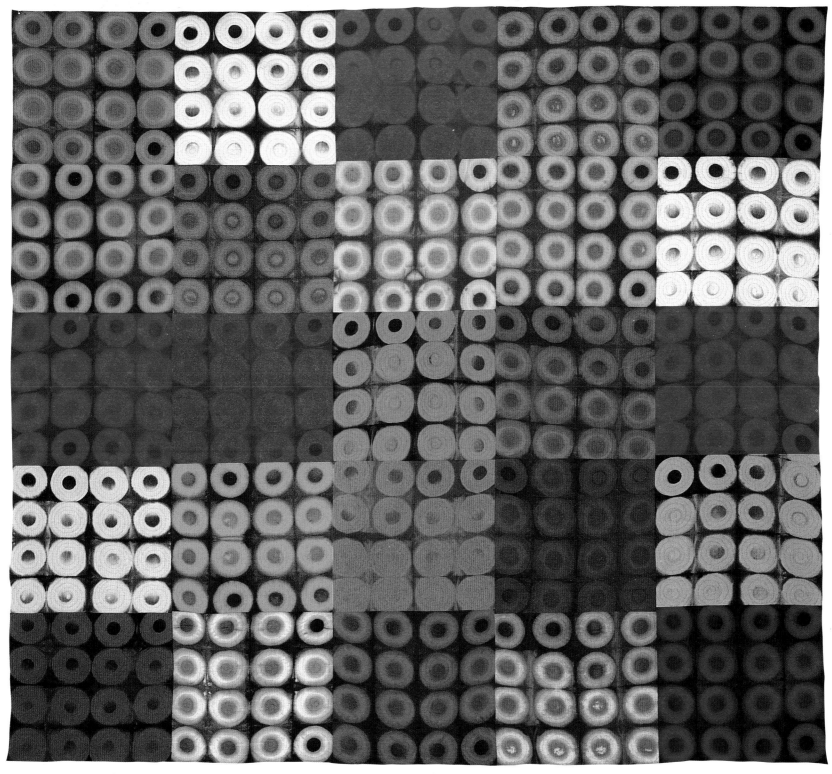

Above: C H I N E S E   S O U L S   # 5

82" x 90"   ©1992 Nancy Crow
Fabrics resist-dyed by Lunn Fabrics.
Machine-pieced by Nancy Crow.
Hand-quilted by Marie Moore with pattern denoted by
Nancy Crow.

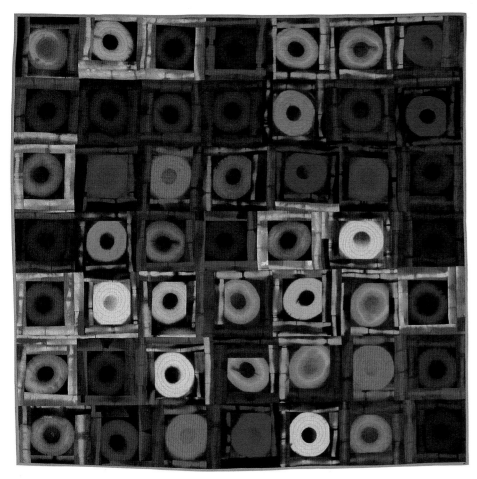

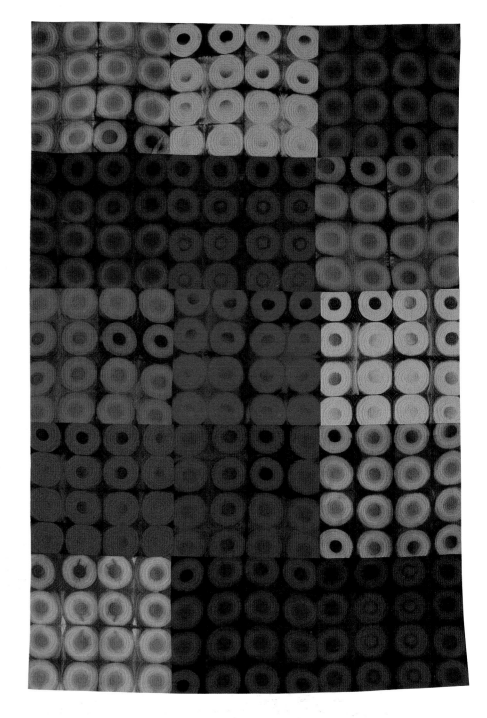

Above Left: <u>C H I N E S E   S O U L S   # 6</u>

45" x 45"   ©1992 Nancy Crow
Cottons hand-dyed by Lunn Fabrics and Nancy Crow.
Machine-pieced by Nancy Crow.
Hand-quilted by Mary Underwood with pattern denoted
by Nancy Crow.

Above Right: <u>C H I N E S E   S O U L S   # 4</u>

42" x 80"   ©1992 Nancy Crow
Fabrics resist-dyed by Lunn Fabrics.
Machine-pieced by Nancy Crow.
Machine-quilted by Anna Mae Gazo with pattern
denoted by Nancy Crow.

Above: CHINESE SOULS #10

56" x 56"   ©1994 Nancy Crow
Curves cut directly and machine-pieced by Nancy Crow.
Hand-quilted by Marla Hattabaugh.

Biography

Nancy Crow
Occupation: Artist
Medium: Quiltmaking
Born: Loudonville, Ohio (1943)
Current Address: 10545 Snyder
Church Road, Baltimore, Ohio
43105 (614-862-6554)

Education:

The Ohio State University-BFA	1965	(Ceramics/Textiles)
The Ohio State University-MFA	1969	(Ceramics/Textiles)
Mexico City College	Winter 1963	(Studied Art)
Columbus Cultural Arts Center	1968-1969	(Studied Weaving)
Penland School of Crafts	Summer 1969	(Studied Weaving)
Arrowmont School of Arts & Crafts	Summer 1972	(Studied Weaving)

Published Books:

Nancy Crow: Improvisational Quilts, 1995, C&T Publishing (800-284-1114)
Gradations: From the Studio of Nancy Crow, 1995, Quilt House Publishing
(800-526-6321)
Nancy Crow: Work In Transition, 1992, American Quilter's Society (800-626-5420)
Nancy Crow: Quilts and Influences, 1990, American Quilter's Society

Book Covers:

Nancy's quilts have appeared on the covers of two of Maya Angelou's books published by Random House:
The Complete Collected Poems of Maya Angelou, 1994
Wouldn't Take Nothing for My Journey Now, 1993

Fabric Designer:

Under the name of NANCY CROW FOR JOHN KALDOR, Nancy designs two fabric collections each year for the international company, JOHN KALDOR, based in New York City, London, Tokyo, and Sydney, Australia. She currently has more than 300 cotton fabrics on the market.

Video:

Nancy Crow/Quilter (1992), produced by Gemstone Productions, Visual Arts Network, P.O. Box 3421, Dayton, Ohio 45401 (513-223-4615)

Exhibitions:

1995 • Solo at The Renwick Gallery of The National Museum of American Art, Smithsonian Institution, Washington, D.C., August 25, 1995, to January 1, 1996
• Solo at The Gallery at Studio B, Lancaster, Ohio, November 12, 1994, to January 7, 1995.
1994 • Invitational: *First Quilt/Last Quilt*, Traveling Exhibition, 1994-1996
• Invitational: *Continuing Innovation in Contemporary American Quilt Art*, Moreau Galleries, Saint Mary's College, Notre Dame, Indiana, September 3-30, 1994
• Shipley Art Gallery, Gateshead, England, June 18 to August 14, 1994
• Textile Museum Max Berk, Heidelberg, Germany, June to July 1994
• Invitational: *Small Works*, The Gallery at Studio B, Lancaster, Ohio, May 28 to July 2, 1994
• Cooper Gallery, Barnsley, South Yorks., England, April 30 to June 12, 1994
• Museum of Applied Arts, Helsinki, Finland, April 20 to May 29, 1994
• Solo at Two Street Studio, Paducah, Kentucky, April 16 to May 14, 1994
• *Solo at University Museum, Indiana University of Pennsylvania, Indiana, Pennsylvania, April 12 to May 14, 1994

• *Solo at The Arnot Art Museum, Elmira, New York, January 14 to April 3, 1994
1993 • Shire Hall Gallery, Stafford, England, November 6, 1993, to January 9, 1994
• *Solo at Museum of the American Quilter's Society, Paducah, Kentucky, September 4, 1993, to January 1, 1994
• Visual Arts Trust Minories Art Gallery, Colchester, England, September 11 to October 10, 1993
• British Craft Council Gallery, London, England, July 15 to September 5, 1994
• *Solo at The American Craft Museum, New York, New York, November 19, 1992 to March 28, 1993
1992 • Invitational: *Craft Today USA*, Sponsored by The American Craft Museum, New York, New York. Traveled throughout Eastern and Western Europe until the end of 1993
• *Solo at The Miami University Art Museum, Oxford Ohio, June 30 to September 27, 1992
• Janis Wetsman Collection, Detroit, Michigan, March 19 to April 11, 1992
• *Solo Exhibition titled *Nancy Crow: Work in Transition* was shown at all the museums marked with an asterisk. The exhibition included 35 quilts dating from 1988-1994

Juror:

1993 *Fiberart International '93*, a juried exhibition designed to encourage innovative work of fiber artists from around the world
1992 *Visions—The Art of the Quilt (1992)*, an international exhibition of contemporary quilts sponsored biennially by Quilt San Diego
The Artist as Quiltmaker V, a biennial competitive exhibition of contemporary quilts opened to artists living in the USA and Canada; sponsored by F.A.V.A.,Oberlin, Ohio

Grants:

1990-91 Major Fellowship of $50,000 from The Ohio Arts Council
1988 Individual Artist's Fellowship, The Ohio Arts Council
1985 Individual Artist's Fellowship, The Ohio Arts Council
1982 Individual Artist's Fellowship, The Ohio Arts Council
1980 Craftsman's Fellowship, The National Endowment for the Arts
1980 Individual Artist's Fellowship, The Ohio Arts Council

Exchange Artist:

Mainland China, Shaanxi Province, sponsored by The Ohio Arts Council, September 1990

Originator of:

1990-Present *Quilt/Surface Design Symposium*, an annual event held the last two weeks of June at The Pontifical College Josephinum, Columbus, Ohio. The purpose of this symposium is to promote quiltmaking as an art form and to provide an intense and in-depth learning experience for serious quiltmakers. Co-director is Linda Fowler, Quiltmaker.

1988-Present *Art Quilt Network*, a group of serious quiltmakers from all over the USA and Canada who meet twice yearly in Columbus, Ohio, at The Pontifical College Josephinum for a weekend retreat that includes discussion and sharing of new work. The *Network* provides a forum for confronting issues dealing with being a serious quiltmaker.

1978-Present *Quilt National*: In 1978, Nancy had the idea of organizing a professional, juried exhibition that would promote contemporary quilts. This project was subsequently undertaken by a large group of volunteers, and a year later in July of 1979, the first *Quilt National* opened in Athens, Ohio, at The Dairy Barn. This exhibition was so successful and so well-attended that it has become a biennial event and international in scope. It is one of the highest quality exhibitions of contemporary quilts held in the United States.

Poster:

1986 In celebration of its 30th year, The American Craft Museum, New York, New York, published a poster using Nancy's quilt, *Bittersweet XIV.* This quilt is now in the collection of The American Craft Museum.

Awards:

1991 *Women Making a Difference,* Sponsored by *The Columbus Dispatch* Newspaper, Columbus, Ohio

1988 *Award for Excellence,* Ohio Designer Craftsmen, "The Best of 1988"

1987 *Award for Excellence,* Ohio Designer Craftsmen, "The Best of 1987"

1986 Recipient of the Ohio Designer Craftsmen *Award for Outstanding Achievement.* It states, "Nancy Crow has been recognized by fellow colleagues and professionals as having made a major contribution to crafts in Ohio through creative and technical excellence, the broadening of the field of knowledge, and in professional accomplishments that will be an enduring inspiration for future generations."

1995 Teaching:

North Country Studio Conference, Bennington College, Bennington, Vermont, January 31 to February 6

Bellevue Community College, Bellevue, Washington, March 2-12

Arrowmont School of Arts & Crafts, Artists' Collaborations (opened only to past faculty), Gatlinburg, Tennessee, May 29 to June 3

The Quilt/Surface Design Symposium 1995, The Pontifical College Josephinum, Columbus, Ohio, June 14 to July 1

Arrowmont School of Arts & Crafts, Gatlinburg, Tennessee, July 15-29

Belle Grove Plantation, Middleton, Virginia, August 2-7

Biennial Conference of the National Surface Design Association, Portland State University, Oregon School of Arts & Crafts and Pacific Northwest College of Art, Tigard, Oregon, August 10-19

Haystack Mountain School of Crafts, Deer Isle, Maine, August 20 to September 2

Quilting by the Sound, Port Townsend, Washington, October 10-15

Collections:

The American Craft Museum, New York, New York
The Museum of American Folk Art, New York, New York
Miami University Art Museum, Oxford, Ohio
The Massillon Art Museum, Massillon, Ohio
Ardis and Robert James
John M. Walsh III
Jack Lenor Larsen
Mark Levine
Mr. and Mrs Tim Keny
Bill and Ruth Lantz
The Electric Quilt Company
Ropes and Gray Law Firm, Boston, Massachusetts
General Foods Headquarters, New York, New York
K-Mart International Headquarters, Detroit, Michigan
E-Z International Headquarters, Saddle Brook, New Jersey
Joan Throckmorton and Sheldon Satin
Dr. and Mrs. Serge Shewchuk
Judge Judy Nicely

39

Other Fine Quilting Books from C&T Publishing:

An Amish Adventure, Roberta Horton
Appliqué 12 Borders and Medallions! Elly Sienkiewicz
Appliqué 12 Easy Ways! Elly Sienkiewicz
The Art of Silk Ribbon Embroidery, Judith Baker Montano
Baltimore Beauties and Beyond (2 Volumes), Elly Sienkiewicz
Beyond the Horizon, Small Landscape Appliqué, Valerie Hearder
Buttonhole Stitch Appliqué, Jean Wells
A Colorful Book, Yvonne Porcella
Colors Changing Hue, Yvonne Porcella
Crazy Quilt Handbook, Judith Montano
Crazy Quilt Odyssey, Judith Montano
Dating Quilts: From 1600 to the Present, A Quick and Easy Reference, Helen Kelley
Dimensional Appliqué—Baskets, Blooms & Baltimore Borders, Elly Sienkiewicz
Elegant Stitches: An Illustrated Stitch Guide & Source Book of Inspiration, Judith Baker Montano
The Fabric Makes the Quilt, Roberta Horton
Faces & Places, Images in Appliqué, Charlotte Warr Andersen
14,287 Pieces of Fabrics and Other Poems, Jean Ray Laury
Heirloom Machine Quilting, Harriet Hargrave
Imagery on Fabric, Jean Ray Laury
Impressionist Quilts, Gai Perry
Isometric Perspective, Katie Pasquini-Masopust
Landscapes & Illusions, Joen Wolfrom
The Magical Effects of Color, Joen Wolfrom
Mariner's Compass, Judy Mathieson
Mariner's Compass Quilts, New Directions, Judy Mathieson
Mastering Machine Appliqué, Harriet Hargrave
The New Lone Star Handbook, Blanche Young and Helen Young Frost
Paper Cuts and Plenty, Vol. III of Baltimore Beauties and Beyond, Elly Sienkiewicz
Pattern Play, Doreen Speckmann
Pieced Clothing, Yvonne Porcella
Pieced Clothing Variations, Yvonne Porcella
PQME Series, Jean Wells
Patchwork Quilts Made Easy, Jean Wells (with Rodale Press, Inc.)
Quilts for Fabric Lovers, Alex Anderson
Quilts, Quilts, and More Quilts! Diana McClun and Laura Nownes
Schoolhouse Appliqué: Reverse Techniques and More, Charlotte Patera
Soft-Edge Piecing, Jinny Beyer
Symmetry: A Design System for Quiltmakers, Ruth B. McDowell
3 Dimensional Design, Katie Pasquini
Visions: Quilts, Layers of Excellence, Quilt San Diego
The Visual Dance: Creating Spectacular Quilts, Joen Wolfrom

For more information write for a free catalog from:
C&T Publishing
P.O. Box 1456
Lafayette, CA 94549
(1-800-284-1114)

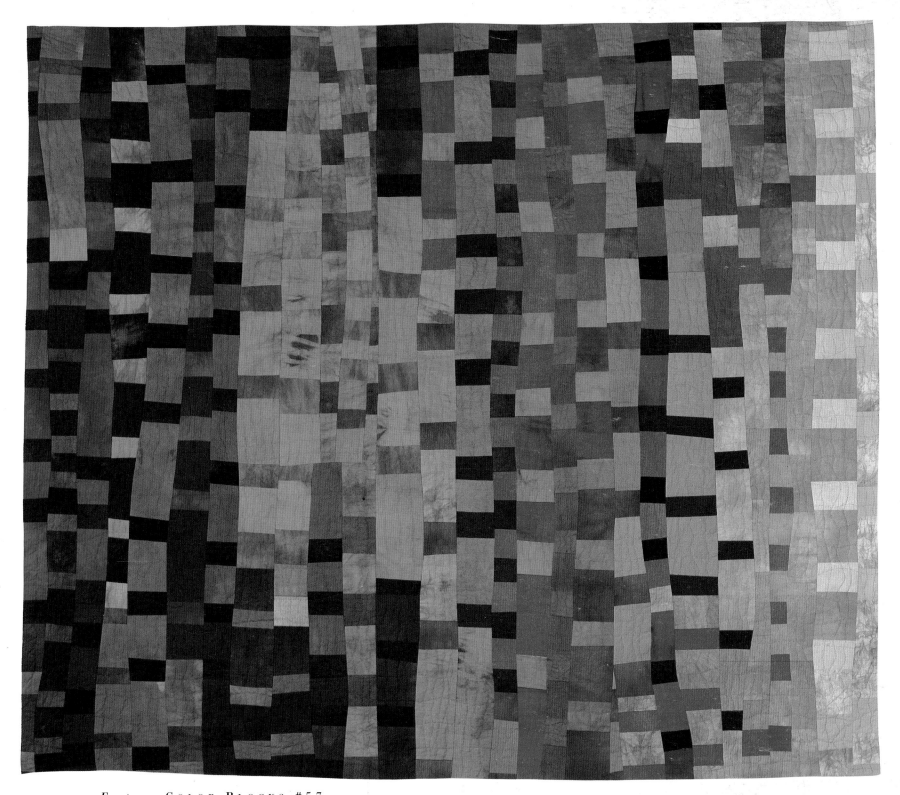

Front cover C O L O R B L O C K S # 5 7

Back Cover 69" x 78"

  Page 2 ©1994 Nancy Crow

  Above: Pima cottons hand-dyed by Nancy Crow.
  Fabrics cut into directly and machine-pieced by
  Nancy Crow.
  Hand-quilted by Marla Hattabaugh.